Little Fish Books about You and Me

British Commonwealth Edition
Published by Scripture Union
London, England.

North American Edition Including Canada
Published by Regal Books
A Division of G/L Publications
Ventura, California, USA

First Edition 1984. Reprinted 1987, 1988

Co-edition arranged with the help of
Angus Hudson, London

Printed and Bound in Great Britain by
Purnell Book Production Ltd., Paulton, Bristol

Little Fish Books about You and Me

I'm Sorry

illustrated by Gordon Stowell

When things go wrong, God,

help me to put them right.

Sometimes I don't help
Mother.

I'm sorry God.

Sometimes I am not kind.

Help me to love others.

Sometimes I don't
share my things.

Help me to be generous.

Sometimes I get too cross.

I'm sorry God.

Sometimes I am careless.

I'll try to do better next time.

Sometimes I forget to do
what Father said.

I'm sorry God.
I'll try to remember next time.

Thank You
that You still love me

even when things go wrong.

Thank You for loving me

...always.

It's fun
Little Fish Books about You and Me

Please God
Little Fish Books about You and Me

God knows
Little Fish Books about You and Me

Thank You God
Little Fish Books about You and Me

Little Fish Books

I'm Sorry
Little Fish Books about You and Me

God loves
Little Fish Books about You and Me

Help me God
Little Fish Books about You and Me

I Like
Little Fish Books about You and Me

bout You and Me